Making Stone

Marie Hartley and Joan Ingilby

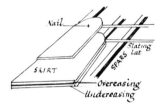

Construction of a roof

Nail

SKIRT

SPARS

Slating Lat

Overeasing
Undereasing

Smith
Settle

First published in 1997 by
Smith Settle Ltd
Ilkley Road
Otley
West Yorkshire
LS21 3JP

ISBN 1 85825 080 3

British Library Cataloguing-in-Publication data:
A catalogue record for this book is available from the British Library.

Set in Monotype Plantin

Designed, printed and bound by
SMITH SETTLE
Ilkley Road, Otley, West Yorkshire LS21 3JP

Introduction

Stonework in the Yorkshire Dales is the dominant feature of the landscape, for wherever you look are to be seen stone walls, barns, cottages, houses, churches, chapels, and in places castles and abbeys. In the Middle Ages, castles were built to protect the domains of the Norman lords, who themselves for 'the health of their souls' gave land to monastic orders which built the abbeys. Richmond Castle was started about 1071, Jervaulx Abbey about 1200, Bolton Priory about 1155, Fountains Abbey about 1135, Middleham Castle about 1170, and Easby Abbey about 1300. Building, especially at abbeys, continued almost up to the Dissolution.

We see these great feats of building, even only as ruins — lofty columns, window tracery, carved capitals, multiple archways, delicate arcading, vaults with ribbed arches — and picture the influx of masons, smiths, stone, scaffolding, lodges (workshops), tools — overseen by the all-important master mason, a wealthy and influential person. On the walls of abbeys and bridges the medieval mason left his trademark, masons' marks. They are reminders of skills inherited by future generations of masons in the dales.

After the Dissolution of the Monasteries, monastic estates were eventually split up, so that the yeomen prospered, and built their long, low, seventeenth century houses, some large, some small, but all with mullion windows, stone-arched fireplaces and dated door-heads. Found the basic construction of houses, barns and walls was the same. Two sides or skins of a wall were built up with a gap in the middle filled with small stones (fillings) and with a 'through' every yard. Through stones span the width of a wall and bind it together. They are dressed so as not to be seen in house walls, but are allowed to project in barns and field walls. Most houses are built with random walling, better ones with dressed stones laid in courses, and a very few are ashlar-faced.

Stones should be walled the way they are laid in the quarry, and every stone should slope outwards and downwards to drain off rain. (Damp walls are the result of inferior workmanship.) A mason can show off with a chimney, which should be three feet high, with a string course to keep off water, and a four inch blocking round the top. We ourselves have seen stone beams in a cart-shed, and chambers over outbuildings, and even bedrooms sometimes had stone floors. Downstairs they were the rule. Laid down in sand and working to a straight edge, flags were placed in rows, and tapped down with a beater.

Roofing with stone slates, so typical of Dales houses, is an art. The slates should diminish in length, width and thickness from the closers at the ridge, three-quarters of an inch thick and nine inches long, to the undereasings and overeasings at the eaves one and half inches thick and thirty-nine inches long. These are spelched, that is tapered off. The slater begins at the eaves, and uses a slate lat and a slate ruler to gauge where the slate lats should come for nailing on the slates. These should overlap three and a half inches and crosslap five inches. No wonder that in roofing it is easy to get wrong. 'A mason's work should be learnt young.'

Lastly, field walls have been described by many people. (See Raistrick's *Pennine Walls*.) They are built with stone at hand, and so exhibit several styles. Gayle near Hawes was the home of many fence wallers, as they were called, at the time of the Enclosure Awards. Most spectacular are walls built straight up a steep hillside, where footing for the waller is precarious and courses have to be laid horizontally. In recent years, many long lengths of roadside walls have been built by county council roadmen. Agricultural shows include competitions for walling in their schedules, and the Yorkshire Dales National Park has adopted a policy of conservation.

Masons in particular have cause to be proud of their handiwork, and wallers no less so. Looking round at the effect of traditional building and walling on the landscape of the Dales, nothing jars.

Acknowledgements

We wish to thank Mr K Peacock for information and for the photograph on page 28 (also used on the cover), Mrs A Holubecki for the loan of the Peacock day-book and for pages 20 and 33, Mr B Alderson for page 40, and Mrs P Dinsdale for dates and names.

The west front of the church at Bolton Priory, described as a master-piece of thirteenth century art.

Building at Fountains
Abbey began about 1135
from stone quarried on
the site. There were also
quarries in Nidderdale
used for shafts.

Bolton Castle, Wensleydale, started about 1370 by Sir Richard Scrope, with Richard Lewyn later as master mason. Leland states that the castle took eighteen years to build.

Kilgram Bridge, the finest of several ancient
bridges in lower Wensleydale. It was described
by Leland in the sixteenth century as the
'great old bridge of stone'. Note the medieval
ribbed arches.

High Hall, Appletreewick, built by Thomas
Craven in 1667. It has a minstrels' gallery.

The porch of Burnsall Grammar School, Wharfedale, possibly the most charming seventeenth century building in the Dales. It was built as a school for poor boys by Sir William Craven in 1603.

Old Cotes, Littondale, dated 1650. It was built on the site of a grange of Fountains Abbey. The bay on the right replacing a barn, is recent.

The doorway of the Folly at Settle, dated 1679, a large, elaborate, three-storeyed house with recessed centre and wings.

A door head at Lumb Farm, Settle.

a range of eighteenth-century buildings in Main Street, Askrigg. Note the sash windows with shallow carved architraves. On the far left, what is now a shop is dated 1770. The rest was built in 1767 by John Pratt, racehorse owner, and is now the Manor House and the Kings Arms Hotel.

Detail of a corner of Winnville, Askrigg, a masterpiece of stonework, built by the masons Philip Dinsdale and his brother in about 1840 for the Winn family. The stonework is watershot, a method of building to turn rain. Note the shape of the quoins.

Double archways in Askrigg Main Street built before 1755. As examples of skilled masonwork, arches are to be seen all over the Dales as arched fireplaces, bridge arches, arches to outbuildings, and lead-smelting hearths.

The upright post is a stoop (gatepost) at one side of a gate. Stoops were sunk two feet six inches into the ground. This example serves as one side of a stile.

Bolton Greets Quarry in Apedale, west of Bolton Castle. It was leased by the Peacock family of stonemasons for nearly 100 years. Here they had a crane, picks, hammers, wedges, and a Lewis to quarry freestone, which was taken away by horse and cart.

Jim Peacock, stonemason of Castle Bolton, using a freestone pick to dress roughly a quoin (corner stone). This was usually done at the quarry.

A mason's tools: steel set square, chisels including pitch tool, punch, boaster, mallet made of beechwood, and hamnmer for use on the punch.

Jim Peacock standing at the banker (workbench) to dress a quoin.
He first applies a steel set square to mark off the size required.

Pitching off the rough with a pitch tool. The same hammer is used
with a punch to reduce to size.

Having used the several tools to dress to size, the mason tools over the quoin with a boaster and mallet.

He uses a one inch chisel with the mallet to chase over.

The mason carves his trademark, based on marks found on stones in Bolton Castle. He prepares a little stone block, and outlines the design in pencil. Then using a small lettering chisel and mash hammer, he cuts the outline.

Jim Peacock making a sundial.

Aysgarth Church, rebuilt in 1864-6.

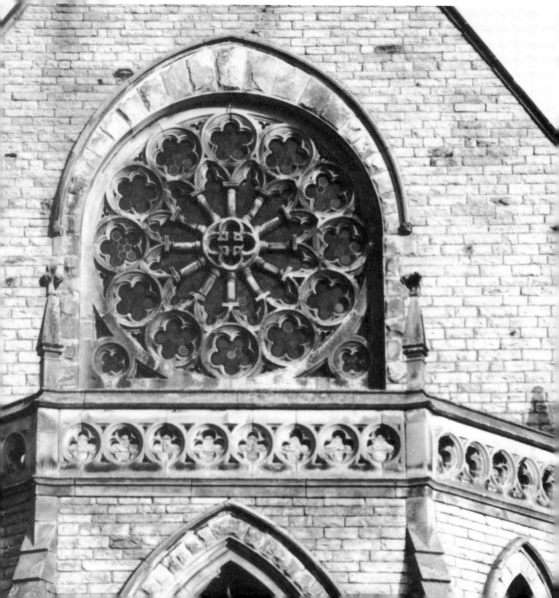

One of several lions carved by James Peacock.

The rose window carved by James Peacock in Leyburn Methodist Church in 1884.

A pair of council houses at Carperby, Wensleydale, designed in the architect's office at County Hall, and built by the Peacocks in 1950. Stone for the quoins came from Bolton Greets, and the rest from New Pasture Quarry, behind Carperby, where stone was once both quarried and mined in quantity.

Tom and Jim Peacock outside one of the council houses.

Keith, Allan and Thomas Peacock repairing the building above Bolton Castle in 1993, used for target practice in the Napoleonic Wars by the Loyal Dales Volunteers.

Stacks of roofing slates at Hill Top Quarry, upper Swaledale. This quarry supplied stone for houses, leadmine buildings, paving, slates and stoops, and is still open. A renowned quarry for roofing slates was Gilbert Scar, near West Scrafton in Coverdale, where stone slates were mined in levels.

The firm of W J Dinsdale and Sons of Gayle, re-roofing a house at Askrigg in 1970. Gayle was noted for its stonemasons and wallers, and this firm was in existence from 1780 to 1992.
Left to right: Arthur Newton, Richard and Thomas Dinsdale, Ken Metcalfe,
Peter Dinsdale and David Iveson.

Taylor Dinsdale of Gayle (whose father and grandfather were stone-masons) re-roofing a house at Askrigg. The gradations of the slates are well shown.

Taylor Dinsdale and his assistant splitting a slate.

N Thwaite and J Percival re-roofing a barn at
Askrigg. The beams and spars had perished,
so the slates were taken off, the woodwork
renewed and the slates replaced. Grants from
the National Park are available for this kind
of work.

County council roadmen building a bridge in the 1950s on a beck at Arngill near Askrigg, where there had been a watersplash.

Taylor Dinsdale's son Allen and grandson John, paving with flags and cobbles at Gayle.
Paving with cobbles was usual long ago, and is still practised at Richmond and Dent.

A well-built barn near Hawes. It is not typical in
plan, but the evenly-spaced rows of throughs
are well seen.

Limestone walls in Malhamdale.

James and Roger Scarr of Coleby Hall, Wensleydale, walling a gap on the farm in the 1950s. Note the through laid across the two sides of the wall.

Colin Rowling of Skipton building a wall of jagged pieces of limestone on Malham Moor. The stone dictates the style of building.

Part of the Deer Park wall above Bolton Abbey,
built about 1650. It is composed of millstone grit
dressed into blocks, hence its appearance.

A remarkably fine
stile in the fields
east of Askrigg,
probably built not
by a waller, but by
Philip Dinsdale,
the stonemason
for Winnville.

An opening made in walls for sheep to pass from one field to another. It could be blocked by a flagstone. It is called a 'cripple hole' in Craven, and a 'thirl hole' in the North Riding dales.